How Artists Use

Shape

Paul Flux

Heinemann
LIBRARY

www.heinemann.co.uk
Visit our website to find out more information about Heinemann Library books.

To order:
☎ Phone 44 (0) 1865 888066
▯ Send a fax to 44 (0) 1865 314091
▭ Visit the Heinemann Bookshop at www.heinemann.co.uk to browse our catalogue
and order online.

First published in Great Britain by Heinemann Library, Halley Court, Jordan Hill, Oxford OX2 8EJ,
a division of Reed Educational and Professional Publishing Ltd.
Heinemann is a registered trademark of Reed Educational & Professional Publishing Ltd.

OXFORD MELBOURNE AUCKLAND JOHANNESBURG BLANTYRE
GABORONE IBADAN PORTSMOUTH (NH) USA CHICAGO

Designed by Celia Floyd
Illustrations by Jo Brooker/Ann Miller
Originated by Ambassador Litho Ltd.
Printed and bound in Hong Kong/China

06 05 04 03 02   06 05 04 03 02
10 9 8 7 6 5 4 3 2 1   10 9 8 7 6 5 4 3 2 1

ISBN 0 431 11521 4 (hardback)   ISBN 0 431 11527 3 (paperback

British Library Cataloguing in Publication Data

Flux, Paul
  How artists use shape.
  1.Proportion (Art) – Juvenile literature 2.Composition (Art) – Juvenile liter
  I.Title
  701.8

Acknowledgements

The Publishers would like to thank the following for permission to reproduce photographs:

AKG, London: pp10, 20, © ADAGP, Paris and DACS, London 2001 p15, Eric Lessing Museo Nazionale Naples p9, ©
DACS 2001 p11, National Gallery of Ireland p19; Art Archive/Tate Gallery, London/ © Succession Picasso/DACS 2001:
p21; Bridgeman Art Library: © ADAGP, Paris and DACS, London 2001 p5, Bolton Museum and Art Gallery,
Lancashire/© Angela Verren-Taunt 2001 All Rights Reserved, DACS p18, Duke of Sutherland Collection/National
Gallery of Scotland p12, St. Peter's, Vatican, Rome p17; Corbis: Philadelphia Museum of Art pp13, 14; Giaraudon: p7;
Henry Moore Foundation: p16; Hermitage, St Petersburg/© ADAGP, Paris and DACS, London 2001: p24; M.C.Escher's
Fishes and Scales c.2000 Cordon Art B.V.-Baarn-Holland: p8; National Gallery, Scotland / Estate of S. J. Peploe: p26;
Tate Gallery: p4; Trevor Clifford: pp28, 29.

Cover photograph reproduced with permission of Bridgeman Art Library.

Every effort has been made to contact copyright holders of any material reproduced in this book.
Any omissions will be rectified in subsequent printings if notice is given to the Publisher.

Contents

Any words appearing in the text in bold, **like this**, are explained in the Glossary.

What is shape?

How many different shapes can you see in this picture? The title suggests we are looking at a room, perhaps the place where the artist works. Some of the squares may be paintings stacked against the wall. Our world is full of shapes: squares, circles, triangles – even some which have no name. Some artists arrange shapes so that we can recognize objects in their paintings. Others use shape to make **abstract** pictures.

Wyndham Lewis,
Workshop,
1914–15

4

Wassily Kandinsky, *Intersecting Lines*, 1923

One way of thinking about a shape is to see it as an
outline, which is then filled with colour. This picture is full of
different shapes. How many can you see? Start at the
bottom right-hand corner and look towards the top left-
hand corner. Although we know paintings cannot move,
the shapes appear to be flying away from us.

Common Shapes

Shapes are everywhere! An artist draws a line, joins it together and fills in the space with colour. A shape is made! Shapes cannot exist on their own, the space around them makes other shapes. A picture is a collection of shapes which fit together, like a jigsaw puzzle. Artists can use shape to make us look at a picture in a particular way.

Leonardo da Vinci,
Mona Lisa, 1503

This is one of the most famous paintings in the world. It is by the Italian artist Leonardo da Vinci. The eyes of the woman seem to follow you as you move around. The **triangular** shape of her head and body lead our eyes upwards. This is why we are always drawn back to look at her face. What is she thinking? People have wondered that for nearly 500 years!

Shapes make space

M. C. Escher,
Fish and Scales,
1959

Shapes affect the spaces around them. In this picture we
first notice the lines of white fish, but look at the spaces
between them. In the middle are two sets of fish scales.
One set moves upwards, the other down. As our eyes
follow them they change into small fish which get bigger.
No space is wasted. Everywhere you look you see fish!

This is a **mosaic**, a picture made from hundreds of small pieces of coloured glass and **marble**. It was made more than 2000 years ago. The Roman artist has shown all the fish and sea creatures that would have lived in the water near the old city of Pompeii in Italy. Although their shapes are fixed, the fish seem to wriggle and sway in the water.

Roman mosaic, Pompeii, Italy

Coloured Shapes

This is one of the earliest paintings ever made. It was painted around 17,000 years ago! The horse has been drawn with a single line and this **outline** has then been coloured in with an unusual **shade** of yellow. Around the young horse are shapes which look like grass, insects, or even birds. Although this was painted long ago, the artist has captured the movement of a real animal.

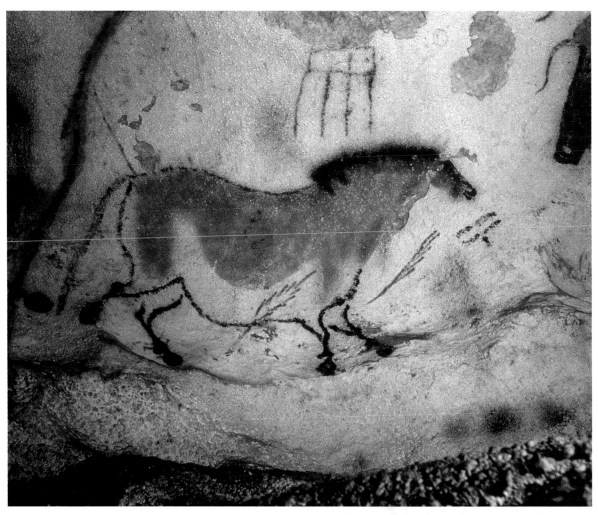

Cave painting, Lascaux, France

Franz Marc, *The Yellow Cow*, 1911

Here is an animal set in an imaginary **landscape** of colourful shapes. This was painted about 90 years ago, much more recently than the horse on page 10. How does this painting make you feel? The mixture of **solid** shapes and bold colours make this a very strong picture. Do you think the cow is running away, or simply jumping for joy?

How Shape is used in portraits

Rembrandt,
Self-Portrait,
aged 51, about 1657

In this **portrait** we see the **solid** shape of the artist looking straight back at us. He looks worried, almost sad. The dark shadows **emphasize** the shape of an unhappy man. Rembrandt painted many portraits of himself. When he was young he showed himself happy and successful. But towards the end of his life, when he was poor, he painted himself like this.

Here the artist has exaggerated shapes to create an unusual effect. The woman's neck and her small head seem carefully balanced. They contrast with the solid shape of her dark dress. Like the *Mona Lisa* on page 7, the **triangular** shape of the figure leads our eyes up to the top of the picture, to the woman's head.

Amedeo Modigliani,
Portrait of a Polish Woman,
1919

How Shape is used in landscape

What could be simpler than a picture of a few houses, bathed in sunlight? The shapes of the roofs mix with the grey light and green trees to make a **landscape** which we can recognize as somewhere real. Yet there is something very special about this painting. The shapes work together to show us a place where people and nature exist side by side.

Paul Cézanne, *Mont Sainte-Victoire*, 1902–06

Georges Braque, *Houses at L'Estaque*, 1908

Only a few years later Georges Braque painted a similar **scene**, but in a very different way. Here the buildings are **solid** shapes, broken up by light and shadow. This **style** is now called **Cubism**, and is seen by many people as the start of modern **abstract** painting. Is this a painting of a real place, or has the artist shown us the changes he sees in one place, at different times of the day?

Solid Shapes – Sculpture

Henry Moore, *Sheep Piece*, 1971–72

Sculpture is often displayed outside, so it has to look good in many kinds of light. This sculpture is called *Sheep Piece* and Henry Moore made it in **bronze** so that it would not fade or rust. Can you see the **outline** of a mother and her baby? The artist has used shape to show the living form of the animals, and wanted the sculpture to become part of the **landscape**.

Michelangelo,
Pieta, 1498–99

Look at the folds of cloth and the way the bodies seem to come to life in this sculpture. It does not look like it is made of **marble**, a very hard rock. The **scene** is one the artist has imagined. Mary, the mother of Jesus, cradles Him in her arms after He has been taken down from the cross. Can you tell what she is feeling?

17

Shapes to make us think

Ben Nicholson was living in Cornwall when he painted this picture. The peaceful **landscape** is made of coloured shapes, each pushing against its neighbour. Is this a real **scene**? If the houses, trees and sky were missing it might look like an **abstract** painting.

Ben Nicholson, *Cornish Landscape*, 1940

**Jan Vermeer,
*Woman
Writing a
Letter with
her Maid,*
about 1670**

Here, light floods in through a window, as one woman looks longingly out and another writes at her desk. What are they thinking about? We are looking at the corner of a room. Although there is a lot of light in the picture, the space seems enclosed by strong shapes. A moment has been frozen in time. Do you feel as if you could reach out and pull the curtain across the room?

Moving Shapes

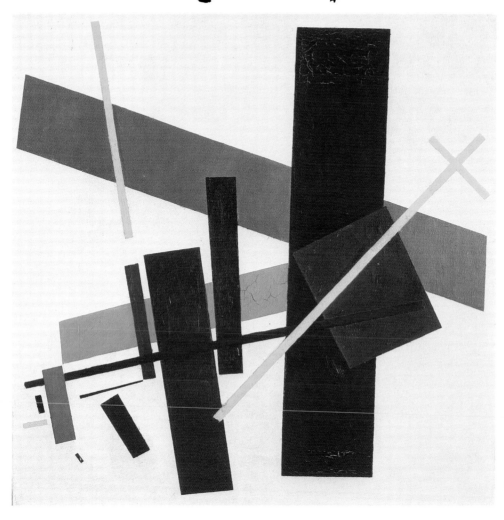

Kasimir Malevich, *Suprematism*, 1915

The Russian artist Kasimir Malevich did not try to show real-life objects in this painting. The shapes and colours work together to create a picture which can make us think of many things. The shapes float in space. Are they moving or fixed in some way? Where have they come from? What does this picture make you think about? Try to draw one like it yourself.

Pablo Picasso,
Weeping Woman,
1937

Pablo Picasso painted this picture while he was angry
about the Spanish Civil War. The woman's head is a
strange shape, because the grief she is feeling has
changed what she looks like. The straight lines of the
background contrast with the twisted shapes of her face
to create a painting full of emotion. There is no colour in
her face and eyes – what do you think this means?

Drawing using Shape outlines

Can you recognize these shapes? Without **shade** and **detail** some shapes can be confusing and difficult to recognize, while others are very easy. Try drawing some **outlines** of objects yourself, or copy some of these. Is it easy to recognize what you have drawn?

Choose an animal and make an outline of it. Copy one from page 22 if you like. Draw another two outlines of the same animal in different positions. Cut the three shapes out and arrange them on a piece of paper. Trace round them, then add some details and colour the spaces between the shapes. Try using different colours until you have a picture you like.

Making a picture using simple shapes

Here is a group of buildings painted in a similar **style** to the pictures by Cézanne and Braque on pages 14 and 15. Look at how the simple shapes of the buildings are given strength by the blocks of colour. The **rectangular** shapes of the houses and their roofs give the picture its **solid** feel. The artist has used little **detail**, but his painting comes alive.

André Derain, *At La Roche Guillon*, 1910

Copy one of these buildings carefully. Colour it in like
Cézanne and Braque, using blocks of the earth colours –
brown, yellow and red. Can you put tree shapes in the
background? Add other shapes until you have made the
picture into a complete **scene**.

Samuel John Peploe,
Still Life, about 1913

A picture of everyday objects is called a still life. Many artists enjoy painting this kind of picture because they can make ordinary things look special. Here the shapes and colours of the background are **repeated** in the objects themselves. This makes it difficult to see where one ends and the other begins.

26

Take three or four simple objects and arrange them in a way that interests you. Draw them as best you can. You may want to try this a few times to get the best view. Now draw lines across and down the page to **divide** the background space, as shown in the example. Can you colour the shapes and background so that the objects really stand out?

Make a picture book

Some of the earliest books were made in China in this way. They are called **concertina books**.

1. Fold a piece of A3 paper into eight rectangles.
2. Open the paper out and fold it again on the longest line.
3. Fold it in half, and then fold one end towards you and the other away from you.
4. Number the pages. Put 1 on the cover, and then 2 to 8 for the rest.

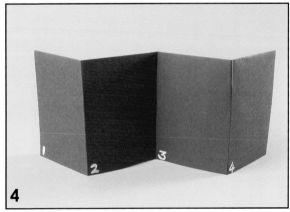

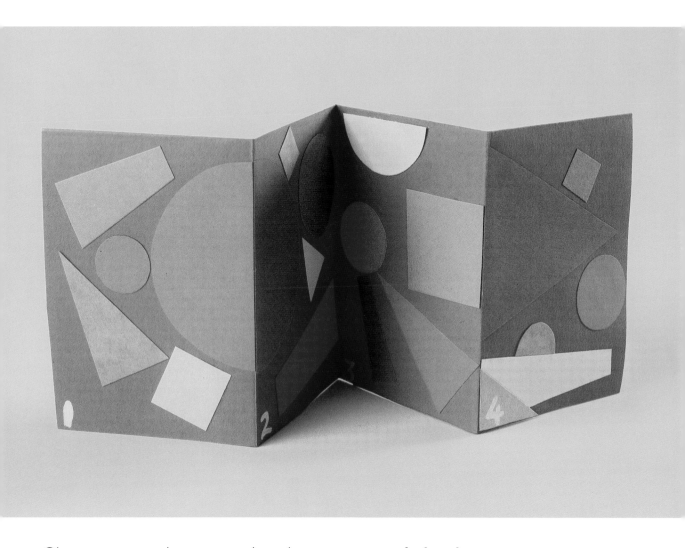

Choose some shapes and make your own **abstract** picture on the first page of your concertina book. Think about how the shapes fit together. Will your picture try to look like something you can recognize in the real world? **Repeat** the picture on the other pages of the book, but move the shapes around and change their colours and size. Now think of a good title for the cover.

Glossary

abstract kind of art which does not try to show people or things, but instead uses shape and colour to make the picture

bronze hard shiny metal used in sculpture, made from copper and tin

concertina book book that folds up like the musical instrument called a concertina

Cubism way of painting which shows one object from different angles or viewpoints

detail a small part of a picture

divide to separate into two or more parts

emphasize to draw special attention to something

landscape picture of natural and man-made scenery, like fields, trees and houses

marble type of stone which many artists like to use for sculpture because it can be highly polished

mosaic picture or pattern made with small coloured stones or pieces of glass

outline line which shows the edge and shape of an object

portrait painting which shows what someone looks like

rectangular in the shape of a rectangle

30

repeat to do something over and over again

scene a landscape or view painted by an artist

sculpture three-dimensional art, made with wood, clay, stone or metal. Can be carved, moulded or glued together.

shade darker or lighter version of a colour

solid something which looks like a real, physical object

style the way in which a picture is painted

triangular in the shape of a triangle

Index